MW00427249

How to Solve Life's Problems

Applying the Ideas of
Spinoza and Gurdjieff

by Gregory Grover

Edited by Lewis Almeida

Almeida Publications
www.wayofspinoza.com

This book was originally a collection of messages which were transcribed from telephone recordings prepared by Mr. Gregory Grover and his students in 1975.

These rules have been established to protect the rights and ownership of Lewis Almeida and Almeida Publications and to ensure that this work is upheld as their own.

Every effort has been made to make this book as complete and accurate as possible. Although the author and publisher have prepared this book with the greatest of care, and have made every effort to ensure accuracy, we assume no responsibility or liability for errors, inaccuracies or omissions.

The purpose of this book is to educate. The author and publisher do not warrant that the information contained in this report is fully complete and shall have neither liability nor responsibility to any person or entity with respect to any loss or damage caused or alleged to be caused directly or indirectly by this book, nor do we make any claims or promises of your ability to generate income by using any of this information.

About Gregory Grover

In 1930, when I was as young college student, I attended a meeting of a group called the Young Idealist Club. Every Saturday evening the members of this group studied literature which stressed individual and mutual ideals: – character development, spiritual thinking, and friendship. The writings of Emerson, Blake, Thoreau, Whitman, Laotzu, Buddha, Lagerlif, van Dyke and others with similar thought were studied, with emphasis on the applications of these ideas to our lives.

After attending several of these meetings, I learned that the Club was a function of The Spinoza Center, which was directed by Dr. Frederick Kettner. In the meetings conducted by Dr. Kettner, I was introduced to the thrilling ideas of Spinoza regarding a full understanding of the human character.

In a matter of months, I was helped to experience some radical character changes. Vast new vistas for inward growth were opened up to me. I was a student in Dr. Kettner's group for 15 years. These years profoundly affected my life and brought to me knowledge, direction, growth, and fulfillment that I had never before envisioned.

In these years I had the opportunity of meeting psychologists (notably Alfred Adler) and spiritual leaders from all over the world, the latter especially from India where Dr. Kettner's writings had been widely reprinted. More particularly, I lived in a community of young men, one whom was born in India and had been nurtured from birth with Eastern thought.

Once a week the community members met to study their own and each other's natures and problems. But our friend from India complained that these studies took him away from his meditations. These experiences brought home to me sharply the limitations of Eastern teachings.

In 1969, I started a group in Los Angeles based on the ideas of Spinoza, who has been called the father of modern psychology. I also used the ideas of Gurdjieff as presented in Ouspensky's writings. Although these latter ideas are limited for my purpose, the psychology of Gurdjieff, as far as it probes, is in harmony with the psychology of Spinoza.

The field of present-day psychology is concerned with a superficial study of human nature. Its basic premise is that man is primarily a biological creation. This concept contrasts with the psychology of Spinoza and Jesus (studied non-theologically) who understood the nature of man through his cosmic origin. According to Spinoza it is impossible to understand the whole nature of man without understanding the nature of God and how man derives from God. This approach I have called COSMIC ETHICS.

The purpose of COSMIC ETHICS is to bring an individual to his highest potential; and his highest potential is that which is innate in him, his deepest essence. In understanding what that is and learning how to work it out, an individual, so to say, understands the mind of God in terms of man's nature.

The various spiritual philosophies also are rather superficial, resulting in a vague mystical experience. My interest has been to work in the direction of Spinoza and Christ to integrate every aspect of human nature: mental, spiritual, emotional, and physical. Above all, my main consideration has been the study of the possibilities of the release of our intelligence capacities.

None of the principles in my research or as presented in these essays are new. But I have probed them to a depth that I have not read about other than in the writings of Spinoza. I have had to develop new words and concepts – the main one being "THE DRAMA IS WITHIN YOU." A grasp of this concept is requisite if growth of real depth is to be achieved.

The publication of this volume was initiated by my students, who wanted to have the ideas that were recorded messages and were heard by telephone when calling a special "Improved Message" number printed for their own use and for the use of others who may find them of interest and value.

About the Editor, Lewis Almeida

I was born into a Mexican-American family. My parents immigrated from Sinaloa and Durango, Mexico. I had 11 siblings, four girls and seven boys. I was the 9th child in a poor family, lost in the maze of orchestrated confusion, with emotional, psychological and some physical abuse.

In 1970, I met my late teacher, Gregory Grover, and he determined that I wasn't a good candidate for the type of work that he was doing. He felt that being from a minority background and being Catholic was not the source or background that would provide the right avenue for intelligent thinking or decision-making. In a nutshell, I was told that I probably would not make it in the Spinoza-Gurdjieff Center in West Hollywood.

Fortunately, I overcame my mental inertia and learned how to examine my nature, and my intuitive intelligence awakened and came to life. I remained in Mr. Grover's group for 24 years.

Now here I am, a private teacher of the philosophy of Gurdjieff and Spinoza, an author, and a public speaker. At times I can't believe it, but I understand how it's possible to make real changes and grow spiritually.

I am honored to have the opportunity to share some of my mentor Gregory Grover's essays and thoughts which will show you how to solve life's problems by applying the ideas of Spinoza and Gurdjieff.

You may reach me at
lalmeida4141@gmail.com.

Growth takes place beyond the present level of our state of being. We must exceed our usual effort level to grow. No growth is possible without outgrowth. But growth does not consist of going against old patterns. We must have some idea of a better pattern of thinking and force our minds to come to the ideas necessary to produce that new level of clarity. The force of inertia must be surpassed.

An individual who has fallen into quicksand will not free himself by struggling against the quicksand. He must get hold of something which is beyond the branch of a tree, a rope that will not give way, and so on; and by holding onto it, pull himself to good ground. We must latch onto some specific idea which involves more thinking activity. As we pull ourselves toward the good ground, we leave behind the swamp. Emerson said, "Hitch your wagon to a star. Keep your seat and there you are."

When we are idealistic, we have a sense of the better but may fail to realize how deeply rooted we are in our old patterns of thinking. A dynamic specific effort is required to come to the realization of our ideals. True ideals are not realized outside ourselves; they are discovered within.

I originated these essays from recorded messages in an effort to reach individuals who have an intense desire and need to grow: individuals willing to put in the required effort, using the tools of knowledge we make available. These essays present, in brief, some of the ideas that I have learned or evolved in the 45 years I have dedicated to an in-depth study of human nature.

The individual seeking answers that he or she has not discovered heretofore may find helpful insights in these essays. But as Gurdjieff has stressed, real growth is possible only for the individual committed to a real work group, properly directed.

"I should like to ask you, nay I do be and entreat you, by our friendship, to apply yourself to some serious work with real study, and to devote the chief part of your life to the cultivation of your understanding and your soul. How, while there is time, and before you complain of having let time and, indeed, your own self slip by."

— *Benedict Spinoza*

How to Solve Life's Problems applying the ideas of
Spinoza and Gurdjieff

Table of Contents

Chapter 1: **Are You a Student of Your Own Nature?**

How do you know things? Have you ever wondered about this? A great deal of our knowledge is based on hearsay. Much of what we believe we have heard from our parents. Many of our values come from them.

Are you a student of your own nature? This is totally different from being a student of things outside yourself. To study math or chemistry is vastly different from studying ourselves. Very few individuals are interested in studying themselves. Therefore, very few people are able to grow.

I shall give you an example. Harold had to have a statement from his father's accountant as a partial requirement in obtaining a contractor's license. He asked his father's accountant what he would charge for preparing the statement. The accountant answered, "Not much." This satisfied Harold. To his surprise, and then anger, he received a bill for $70.00 from the accountant for a brief amount of work.

Harold called his father to complain about the bill. The father also thought the accountant's charge was high, but said to

1

How to Solve Life's Problems applying the ideas of
Spinoza and Gurdjieff

Harold, "If you have learned a lesson from this, the $70.00 will have been well spent." His father has expressed this idea on several past occasions, but Harold had not learned anything from these experiences.

I suggested to Harold that he get a pencil and paper and begin to really study his nature. Actually he has paid $70.00 for a course in the school of life. But if he does not learn anything from it, he will have wasted $70.00 and in the future he will have similar experiences. In order to learn about himself from this experience, Harold has to force his mind to come to new ideas. Memory doesn't help here, because in his memory storeroom there are no answers.

There is in all of us, as in Harold, a tremendous inertia in our minds. In order to deal with problems concerning our nature, we must face far more inertia than when thinking about things outside our nature with which we are not emotionally involved. You have probably heard the saying that if we do not learn from history, history will repeat itself. This is true of personal history as well as world history.

Chapter 2: **Belief in Free Will Is a Mental Mispronunciation**

We know what mispronouncing means in regards to words. There is also mispronouncing of ideas. A confused idea is mental mispronunciation. Just as there are words that are commonly mispronounced, there are commonly mispronounced ideas.

One of the most frequent examples of mental mispronunciation is belief in free will. The mind believes in free will because it does not understand that the cosmos operates through fixed laws. When you desire, think about, or do something, do you believe free will is present? If so, you are ignorant of the laws that are operating. If you are angry at the action of someone else and attribute free will to that person, then you do not understand that the other person had no choice.

The illusion of free will is the basis for our emotions of anger, blame, envy, etc. If you think deeply enough about any action, you will uncover the cosmic laws that are the basis of this action. You will then realize that what has happened could not have been otherwise.

There is a French proverb that to understand all is to forgive all. This is only partially accurate because when we understand, there is nothing to forgive. Even the word "forgive" suggests that something could have been different.

When you understand the necessity behind something, all emotions will disappear. To be free is to understand, and to understand means that you have grasped consciously the fact that everything that occurs, occurs because of the fixed and eternal laws of the cosmos.

Chapter 3: **Concentrating on Specifics to Develop Clear Thinking**

The third of the three disciplines for the development of consciousness that we are studying and applying in our group is the concentration on specifics. The conscious mind is constituted mainly of simple, clear and distinct ideas. The confused mind is made up of blurred ideas – ideas that are mixtures that are blends of two or more partial ideas.

But the difficulty is that we are so accustomed to thinking in a confused manner that often we are not aware that we are confused. We accept our confusions as though they were clarities. If you examine your thinking with care, you will begin to discover in how many areas it consists of blended ideas – not clear ideas. You will begin to observe how much of your life is based on hit-or-miss efforts rather than clear thinking which is based on a study of the specific realities involved.

Your thinking can be improved by beginning to work with simple realities and concentrating on them. The purpose is to help you lead a life based on reason – on clear thinking. Take some small act, something simple, and apply your mind to study it in detail. For example, the next time

6

you open your door lock, observe how the key operates and how the lock opens. Don't do it haphazardly. By concentrating on a small deed of this kind, you will gradually train your mind to think specifically rather than generally or vaguely.

Chapter 4: Conscious Effort Is an Inner Requirement

Our being has an effort requirement. When we apply this effort from within our being in adequate directions, we experience a sense of fulfillment. The motivation for this effort comes from within us. We use ourselves, expend and extend ourselves, for our own sake. If we merely apply effort from an external motivation, we do not experience this fulfillment. The effort must be expended for our own sake. It is part of our mission to apply this effort with consciousness: conscious that we are applying ourselves for our own sake; wrong motivation cannot produce fulfillment.

When you are applying adequately-motivated effort, there is an inner sense of rightness, adequacy, peace, wholeness and joyousness. When the motivation is wrong, there are many signals which tell us this. If we experience inferiority, superiority, lack of self-respect, emotional dependence, lack of confidence, emptiness, disappointment, depression, anger, envy, jealousy or blame, we are not expending the inner effort needed to nourish our being. If you look toward others for respect, affirmation or approval, then you are not providing your own: you are then parasitic.

The majority of individuals use only a tiny portion of the effort needed to nourish themselves inwardly. There are two aspects to whatever you do – the external and your inner being. If you concentrate on the external and are not conscious of yourself, you will remain inwardly unfulfilled. Practice being conscious of yourself in whatever you do and make this consciousness a priority in whatever you are doing. Expend more and more effort from within yourself for your own sake and you will begin to feel you are on the right path, for you now experience yourself intuitively.

Chapter 5: Creating Our Existence Anew

Whenever you have an experience, a memory of it follows. The experience may have been a product of the activity of your intelligence, but the memory is passive. Think of a waterfall and a picture of the waterfall: the waterfall is dynamic; the photograph is passive.

The growth-directed individual lives with an active intelligence; but there is a tendency in us, after some positive experience, to dwell on the memory of it – passively coasting. The memory has a value when used as a tool by the intelligence. But in itself the memory is not a dynamic experience, even though it may recall the emotions we felt in the actual experience.

If you find yourself dwelling on memories, turn your mind to the present and put in effort to create a new experience now. Goethe phrased this well when he stated that we must create our existence anew each and every day. Activate your intelligence: Begin again in the now and go toward the future; leave the past alone, no matter how wonderful. If you attempt to learn something from it for the sake of the future then you are using it as a tool. Disengage yourself from the past; turn your mind to the reality of the now: Go ahead! If you do not succeed, begin again. Beware, do not let the lack of instant results deter you. You gain something within yourself by the very effort itself.

We feed ourselves by our efforts; therefore, we are never really fed by anything external to us to which we respond passively. We are truly fed and fulfilled by the continuously new, renewed and stronger efforts that we apply in any experience. Then we learn that real confidence comes from the fact that we have gained the ability to apply ourselves to every experience or problem we face.

Chapter 6: Creating Your Inner Destiny with New Beginnings

Do you understand the "Begin Again" principle? Do you know how to begin again at any moment and leave the past behind, how to disengage your mind from old negative memories and live in the present, going toward a better state and a better future? Are you chained to the past, to regrets, shame and guilt, which is rooted in the illusion that you have free will?

To begin again you must have some degree of "I" consciousness, awareness that you can create your inner destiny. Destiny is not an outer condition; it is an inner state of mind. Fate is to be in the world and of the world. Destiny is to be in the world but not of the world. A conscious pursuit of destiny is to create a kingdom within ourselves.

When you find yourself bogged down in some inner confusion, have the courage to think and to say to yourself, "I shall begin again – Now!" You must train your mind to think in this way again and again and again in specific experiences. To affirm new beginnings intellect-tually is useless, and to have merely an emotional feeling about beginning again is equally futile.

You must start to think in terms of beginnings again with your whole being. If you believe it is not possible to think in this way, then you have fallen victim to the trap described by Spinoza as a law of human nature: If we think something is impossible, then it is impossible. Much of our hopelessness is based on the fact that we have accepted the premise of impossibility.

Train your mind to make a new beginning now and then. Don't expect instant results. Every effort will gradually strengthen your mind, until at some point you will have developed enough strength to. find yourself in that miraculous state where you are really free from the past moment, past memory, or even a long ago past. You'll find your mind fresh, free and future-directed. There is no end to the new beginnings you can make. Begin again and go ahead to a new and better future.

Chapter 7: **Discriminating Between Your Intelligence and Memory**

Are you becoming aware that almost everything you do is based on responses of memory patterns to present problems, situations, circumstances and the like?

We are all programmed early in life with different patterns that become embedded in our memory banks. The result is that almost all of our mature existence has been predetermined, so that instead of living spontaneously in the now we are responding mindlessly; that is, without consciousness, to various external stimuli. But because we are unaware of these deeply-rooted patterns in our memory, we are under the illusion that we make choices out of free will.

When you begin, dimly at first, to recognize the great difference between your intelligence and your memory, your intelligence will slowly and gradually become activated so that you will be able to begin responding to problems and circumstances by asking yourself real questions. By asking yourself, "WHAT DO I THINK ABOUT THIS NOW?" you are not merely responding from pre-set patterns.

You will consult your memory and use it as a tool, and then make decisions based on the best thinking you can do now.

This consulting of your intelligence will slowly strengthen it, and you will enter on the training path needed to discriminate between your dynamic intelligence and your passive memory. Then a process of growth will begin in your intelligence. In time you will discover yourself becoming more alive and you will experience a new kind of joy based, not on externally-produced sensations, but on the inner sense that you are really on the path of true self-fulfillment.

Chapter 8: **Factualizing Our Confusions into Simple Ideas**

Have you ever gone through the experience of having a stuffed-up drain in your kitchen sink or bath tub? What causes this blockage? Waste items which would easily flow through the drain become fused together and clog the drain pipe so that all waste which is then put into the drain begins to back up. This fusing together is a "confusion." If the confused mass is broken into small pieces, the flow of water will once again return to normal.

Similarly, when our mind becomes loaded with fragmented ideas, these ideas fuse together and our mind becomes confused. We then experience the pain of intense confused emotions and our lives become confused.

Clear and adequate ideas flow through our mind without blocking the process of thought. Therefore, to unblock our minds we must break our confusions into the specific elements. The flow of thought will then proceed adequately and we will experience an increasing sense of inner adequacy and well-being.

Here are some of the elements that will be found in a confused idea. First there are real physical facts; write these down. Then there are emotions. Observe and write down what emotions you experience. The more common ones are hope, fear, ego, inferiority, superiority, hatred, envy, self-pity and jealously. If you become aware of hope, factualize the hope and un-blend it from other emotions, judgments, and so on. Observe the hope by itself. If you judge yourself, you now have confusion. The judgment must be observed factually and separated from the emotions.

Simple ideas are always clear. Therefore, in simplifying our thinking, the confusion disappears. You work on yourself in this way; your mind will gradually gain more and more strength and clarity.

Chapter 9: **Five Steps for Studying and Solving Problems**

Here are some keys that may help you in studying and solving problems:

Step 1: Affirm that an unsolved problem does exist.

Step 2: Admit that you are ignorant about an adequate solution to the problem.

Step 3: Remember that it is possible to come to a clear idea about anything.

Step 4: Activate your mind by being in wonder about the problem.

Being in wonder is necessary for you to begin to study the problem. The writing discipline is a highly-effective tool. Get pen and paper and begin writing whatever thoughts come to you about the problem. If you can be open-minded, your mind will become active and gradually ideas and insights will begin to develop. Discipline yourself to reach for new ideas and write these down as they come to you.

Step 5: Decide whether the problem is totally within you, both within you and external to you, or totally external.

Is the problem totally within you? Example: You feel depressed.

Is the problem dual – both within you and external to you? Example: You have a toothache. You are afraid you may lose the tooth. The fear is an internal problem. The outer aspect is that you do not have a satisfactory dentist. How can you find one?

Or is the problem totally external? Example: Your boss is temperamental. He does not touch any emotions in you. However, you have to learn to understand him in order to work adequately with him. Find out which of these aspects apply to you. In the case of the dual problem, study each aspect separately. If you blend them together, no solution can be achieved.

If you have any emotions about the problem, this is due to confused thinking. Nothing external can affect you emotionally unless your thinking is confused.

Chapter 10: Forcing Our Mind into Simple Ideas

In the last several days some of our members have raised questions about the idea of forcing ourselves. The fact is that we must force ourselves to grow inwardly. The belief that we grow easily and without great effort is an illusion that indicates one's ignorance about human nature. But it is possible to force ourselves in the wrong way.

Our motive determines the adequacy of our self-forcing. If we force ourselves to obtain the approval of others, to be liked by others, or to conform to our peer group, the motive is wrong. If we force ourselves purely for our own sake, because our intelligence indicates to us areas of confusion or higher possibilities, then the motive is adequate and we are guided by our reason or intuition into the proper channels.

What do we force? Our minds! We must force our minds into more activity so that we are motivated by new insights rather than by old memory patterns. It is well said that we are creatures of habit, and habits makes us into machines. When we activate our intelligence, we cut through the bonds of our memory patterns and free ourselves from old habits. We concentrate on situations and problems in order to come to ideas. Our standards arise from our clear thinking: almost all of our present standards are borrowed from others. The new standards are thoroughly in harmony with our essential nature.

Spinoza found himself in a life and death struggle when he decided to live a conscious life, for he had to change old values and ideas. The inertias of our mind are enormous, and the conditioning which has led us to depend on approval from other people is deeply rooted. Real growth is possible only when we force ourselves to break through our conditioned thinking and really learn how to be guided by our understanding. The following A.B.C. would apply:

A. I help myself
B. I force myself
C. I lift myself up

Chapter 11: **Harmonizing the Thinking 'I' and the Doing 'I'**

There is a tendency in us, as Ouspensky explains in *In Search of the Miraculous,* to think of ourselves as being a whole individual, when in fact there are many 'I's in us. I shall now speak about two 'I's. There is a thinking 'I' and a doing 'I'.

Again and again thoughts come to us which we desire to enact, but we cannot do so. The result may be frustration or depression. We feel split.

If you realize that these two 'I's do exist, then you can begin to study how to harmonize them. The doing 'I' acts from old memories. We are indeed creatures of memory habits until we begin to activate our intelligence. When our intelligence is operative, then we begin to think. When thinking commences, we can see things in terms of problems rather than through old memory attitudes. When we can problemize, we are creative. When we are creative, problems become the food through which we grow in understanding.

When our intelligence is active, we can then apply a four-step formula to harmonize the thinking 'I' and the doing 'I'. First we observe that the two 'I's are different, and we pay attention to the thinking 'I' as a distinct 'I'. Then we begin to wonder about it. This activates the intelligence. Without wonder we live on the basis of memories. With active wonder we live in the present, constantly going ahead to clearer thinking. And this is what growth is all about. Wonder activates the intelligence, and ideas begin to emerge – some of these ideas being intuitive and others arising from reason. The fourth step is free activity which takes place when the thinking 'I' and the doing 'I' are harmonized and become 'one'.

Chapter 12: **Strong Effort Is a Requirement for Fulfillment**

One of the requirements for fulfillment is that we live with strong effort, effort expended for the sake of satisfying the requirements of our inner being. If we do not feed ourselves with enough effort, we are inwardly dissatisfied and blame conditions for this dissatisfaction.

This morning I spoke to Theodore, a member of our group, who related his fears that a few physical deficiencies might make him unattractive to girls. When I suggested that these deficiencies could be remedied, he replied that he would then feel unnatural because he really wouldn't be himself. Obviously, it was illogical that he would speak about these physical lacks and then avoid doing anything about them. This simply proved that he was using these deficiencies an excuse to cover up some deeper problems.

We then studied the idea that he was afraid of competition with other men and was using his deficiencies as a buffer to ease the pain of rejection. But as we worked toward the idea that the drama is within us, we were now able to uncover the real problem. Theodore's inner being was demanding that he live with much more effort expended for his own sake, and not because of external motivation, that is, to get approval from others, to be superior to others, or for monetary gain.

Effort must be expended for the sake of exercising our being. Theodore's parental environment encouraged indulgence rather than the expending of effort, and this was the source of his inferiority. The problem of relating to girls only served as an opportunity to express, in a camouflaged way, the unfulfilled requirements of his inner being. The problem in Theodore had nothing to do with external circumstances. It proved once again that our real problems are within us. The drama is indeed within.

Chapter 13: Interpreting the Messages from Our Inner Intelligence

The individual who has a genuine desire to grow must discriminate between the real problems in his nature and the symptoms of problems. If we deal only with the symptoms, no growth will occur and much time and effort are wasted.

William and I studied an experience that he had while taking measurements on a pier. William believed that the pier manager did not respect his efforts and he felt the pain of rejection. He has had similar experiences on other occasions.

Joan told me about her envy she experiences when a woman friend was given an art assignment for which she was to be paid $1,500. Yesterday our group had an outing in the mountains. Ralph drove the car in which I was riding. He went through a good deal of pain because he felt I would be critical of his driving adequacy.

Each of these individuals had outwardly different problems. And yet, inwardly their problems had a common pattern. The awakening intelligence in each of them was counseling them about the growth direction. Each of them had buffered the voice of his or her intelligence. But their intelligence, refusing to be disregarded, manifested itself in an indirect fashion.

Although William felt rejected by the pier manager, it was the voice of his intelligence which was rejecting many of his efforts. Joan's envy was really the voice of her own intelligence calling upon her to live a more spontaneous life rather than the imitative existence she pursued. And Ralph's intelligence was advising him that he had to put in more adequate efforts in his activities, whether in driving or in anything else.

The essential intelligence in each one of us is the only true authority to follow. The purpose of our group is to help each individual become aware of this voice within, to learn how to interpret the messages that come from our intelligence, and to discriminate between this living voice and the voices of our dead memory patterns that mechanically direct our lives.

Chapter 14: **Living in the Now**

Today, a man who I know and who I'm involved in inner growth told me that he had made an unfortunate investment in real estate and had lost a great deal of money. He had planned to retire soon but now can't follow through with his plan. "What would you do in this circumstance?" he asked. After studying his situation, I told him that he was experiencing the emotion of remorse and this was making his inner situation miserable because the past can't be changed. Remorse exists only in our imagination. It is not realistic thinking.

I told him that I endeavor to live in the present. To do so I must let go of the past and begin again. He could see the logic of it but, of course, intellectual affirmation alone does not overcome the emotions. Emotions are only overcome by contrary and stronger emotions. As Gurdjieff would say, we are attached to our suffering and can't seem to let it go. I suggested that he consider what could be done right now and he responded to this. He told me he had made the investment at the suggestion of a friend. He could see that it took less effort to believe in the friend's counsel than to put in the effort to research the investment for himself.

Spinoza states that remorse only derives from rashness; that is, through blind hope we do something about which we are in doubt. Then comes the companion emotion of repentance if the result is bad. If you have put in an adequate effort in thinking through some plan or act and the results are unsatisfactory you will not experience regret. Regret arises in part from the intuitive sense that we did not apply adequate thought to some action. The pain of regret actually arises from this sense of inner inadequacy rather than from the external error of judgment.

Chapter 15: Activity in Simple Realities Overcomes Complaining

One sacrifice that must be made in the transition from childhood to maturity is giving up complaining. Complaining is a protest against reality. Ordinarily it accomplishes nothing. However, in our imagination we seem to feel better if we complain. Maturity means seeing problems with realism. In accepting problems and applying our intelligence to solve them, we are given the opportunity for growth.

When we complain, we reject the problems confronting us. Complaint is a buffer against reality. It is associated with self-pity, emotional dependence and avoidance of responsibility. It arises because we are not putting in the required effort to solve a problem. It is rooted in wishing for something rather than working for it.

Whenever you find yourself in a complaining mood, you are passive. If you become aware of this tendency, use it as a signal to put in a new effort in facing some problem. Activate yourself. Compel yourself to become involved with some reality. When you are active, you cannot be in a complaining mood.

Do something positive. It may be something as simple as washing dishes or sweeping the floor. However, do something positive! Then you will be on the way to overcoming your passivity, your state of helplessness. Then your intelligence will begin to be activated. You will gain the sense of yourself and of your power to apply yourself to problems and solve them.

Affirm again and again that you can activate yourself. Remember that more time and effort are needed than you may have planned. So begin at the beginning and continue to apply yourself to your problem. Think of your effort rather than the problem. In working on the problem, remember: "I am working on the problem," with the emphasis on the 'I' rather than on the problem. Then you will gain the sense of yourself and not get lost in the problem.

Chapter 16: **Our Inherent Growth Force**

How do we grow inwardly? Let us take as an example how we grow in physical strength. The weight lifter sets for himself a goal beyond his present capacity. Suppose he has reached a 200-pound limit. Now he decides to reach a 250-pound capacity. He strains his muscles to lift a heavier weight than ever before. As he continues his exercises, his muscles are forced to adapt themselves to the increased load. The self-preservative force – the conatus – which is present in all living things compels the muscles to increase in strength. Inwardly the same phenomenon occurs. If we set ourselves the goal of working out some problem which we could not deal with before, our understanding is similarly stretched and new ideas come to us.

In lifting weights, we decide to lift the heavier load and apply ourselves to the task. But the body accomplishes the growth through its own mechanisms. Similarly, the understanding is exposed to a more difficult problem. We apply thought to the problem. But the real work of growth is achieved by a growth force that is inherent in our deeper intelligence. Our conscious effort is but a small part of the process. Deeper resources within us take over and work in a workshop deep within us that is beyond the reach or comprehension of our more superficial intellect.

If we believe that the awareness we possess is all that is possible, our growth will be minimal. We must have the intuitive faith that this deeper intelligence within us must be allowed to digest the problem and, in its own time, produce insights which our aware mind can grasp. Evidence of this process is observed when an idea or solution to some problem comes to us unexpectedly when we do not seem to be thinking about the problem.

The more we understand this aspect of growth, the more we set it into operation by feeding problems into our minds just as we put food into our mouths and chew and swallow it. Only when we understand how this process operates can we achieve real growth.

Chapter 17: **Speaking Simply, Thinking Clearly**

Simple ideas are the basis of clear thinking. The clarity of your thinking will be expressed in the way you speak. Are the thoughts you express simple or complex? Study your verbal self-expression. Using a tape recorder will be helpful. Also study the way others speak; see if your thoughts and their thoughts are simple.

Let us take an example: Joe says to Frank, "You wouldn't like to go to the movies, would you?" This is an example of complicated thinking. Another example: Joe says to Frank, "Have you thought of that terrific picture they're showing at the Mann Theater in Westwood? Tonight's the last chance to see it; it would be a shame to miss it. Henry saw it and raved about it. I think you'll regret it if you don't see it. How about going?"

Simple thinking is straightforward; it's not manipulative. Example: Joe says to Frank, "Tonight is the last night the latest Harry Potter movie is playing at the Mann Theater in Westwood. I plan to see it and I would enjoy your company if you would like to see it. It had excellent reviews. Henry said he enjoyed the movie very much." Joe speaks for himself as an individual and allows Frank to make his own decision. This is mature and simply communicated. Listen to yourself. Are your thoughts expressed simply and directly? If they are clear, they can be expressed simply. If they are complex, your speech will be complex. Working at speaking simply is a wonderful discipline for helping yourself to think clearly.

Chapter 18: **The Struggle for Essence**

There is a vast difference between the struggle for existence and the struggle for essence. As human beings, we are all involved in the struggle for existence. Very few of us are involved in the struggle for essence. The struggle for essence begins when we start to discriminate between our intelligence and our old memory patterns.

These memory patterns are as old as we are. They are deeply entrenched. They dominate and determine our existence and our future, while our intelligence is dormant. We must force it into action. We must compel ourselves to ask as frequently as possible, "What do I think?" The memory will tend to give answers, but they are only old answers. The real intelligence is spontaneous; it relates to the now.

The struggle for essence is the struggle to activate the intelligence and then to follow its path rather than the memory path. When you live from your intelligence, life is fresh, free, fulfilling and joyful. When you are guided by your intelligence you can have dynamic, non-bargaining relationships with other individuals who are also intelligence-guided. In fact, relationships between and among individuals who are not guided by voices of intelligence are sleep relationships; therefore, asleep people live asleep lives and relate to others in sleep.

The goal and the direction of a real study and work group is the endeavor to wake up, to awaken our intelligence.

Chapter 19: **You Are Not Your Memory Patterns**

William Wordsworth, the English poet, wrote a sonnet in which the following line appears: "A pagan suckled in a creed outworn."

The memory patterns which rule our lives are for the most part aptly described by this line, and we have indeed been suckled in creed outworn. If you examine the quality of your life honestly, you will have to affirm that the creed by which you were raised is not in harmony with the realities of the character and life that you desire and aspire to become. You will have to develop a whole new creed as different from your old creed as day is from night.

To accomplish this, you must understand that your old creed, made up of the memory patterns which direct your existence, is totally inadequate when it comes to the real meanings and values in your life. Your memory patterns may be adequate enough in regard to ordinary realities – how to walk, to talk, or even how to reach the moon. But this has no relationship to fulfilling the requirements of your essential character.

You Are Not Your Memory Patterns!! These patterns were formed long ago when you were very young and lacked the intelligence capacity to evaluate the false premises which you accepted as realities. Begin to distinguish between your now self (that is, your intelligence) and your old self (that is, your outworn memory patterns). As you begin to be guided by your now-intelligence rather than by your old patterns, you will discover that you indeed have to go through a great rebirth process.

If you are willing to embark on this project, if inwardly there is something young and dynamic, something in your being that is not already crystallized, then a new character may be developed in you. This is the work of our group in which the active students are participating and creating for themselves an inner life totally different in quality than their former existence.

Chapter 20: **Breaking Through Our Fear of Judgment**

Several days ago, in a private meeting, I met with Josephine and Elizabeth who are members of our group. Josephine was going through an intense struggle. She was resistant to talk about it because she was afraid of the judgment she believed we would have of her. Finally she told us something she had done which was the cause of her intense emotion.

Neither Elizabeth nor I judged her. We studied what she had done and encouraged her to think more deeply about it. Actually Josephine's action required some courage. Her fear of telling us about it was not fear of our judgment but her fear of really thinking about what she had done, for then she would have to face the confining thoughts she had about herself and break through to larger ideas.

When we are young, before our intelligence can develop, we construct premises based on fear in order to protect ourselves. Our fear premises are pickets which become picket fences as a means self-protection. But as we mature, these fences become our prisons.

Josephine found her picket fence too confining. She intuited the need to break through it, but was afraid to think about it consciously. Her fear of our judging her was the fear within herself of having to face her imprisoning premises. But there was another part of her that wanted to break through. As we studied her situation, she succeeded in making some steps in the direction of inner freedom.

Chapter 21: **The Drama Is Within**

On November 24th, 1975, is the 343rd birthday
anniversary of Benedict Spinoza, whose comprehension of human nature, as detailed in his
writings, has been paralleled only by the non-
theological Christ, and whose teachings encom-
pass the principles upon which our group is
based.

This article will examine further the idea that
the drama is within us. At a project meeting,
William found himself competing with Joseph to
have his ideas accepted for this particular project.

As we studied William's nature, William
would give only a mediocre or modest effort to
developing his thoughts. He sensed that Joseph
was more adequate in his thinking. This caused
William pain, not because Joseph's ideas were
more thoroughly thought through, but because he
was inwardly dissatisfied with the quality of his
own thinking.

Contact with Joseph compelled him to be
aware of his own inertias. He found himself
resistant to applying the effort that his inner
intelligence required to satisfy an inner standard.

His desire to compete with Joseph was a way
of not facing his inner debt to himself. If he
would prove himself superior to Joseph by having

42

his ideas accepted in preference to Joseph's, this would produce a self-complacency and he would then not have to face the inner requirements that he resisted.

Chapter 22: **Testing Our Ideas in the Marketplace**

An innate requirement of our mind is to come
to certainty about any idea that we may have.
When certainty is attained we are at peace about
that idea. If we are uncertain, we experience
mental pain which is paralleled by physical pain.
With most ideas, a considerable work effort is
needed to bring them to the state of clarity; that
is, the state of adequacy which is accompanied by
certainty. But there is a strong tendency in us to
accept ideas, feelings or impulses as they come to
us. This is why the quality of our lives is so poor.

Due to our subjective tendencies, it is
extremely difficult to examine our ideas
objectively. This is one of the reasons why
growth can take place only in a group. For in a
group we can share our ideas with others and
learn to examine them to discover what is
adequate in the ideas and what needs further
development. Our ideas are then (to use a popular
phrase) tested in the marketplace.

If you are interested in growth, which simply
means improving your understanding, you must
discipline yourself to allow your ideas to be
tested in the marketplace, to hear how others
respond to your ideas. If you find yourself with a

resistance to expose your thinking, this is because intuitively you sense the un-clarity, the uncertainty, of your thinking and are afraid to hear what others think, because then you would be compelled to rethink your ideas, re-examine your premises and discover your character weaknesses. This will require a tremendous sense-of-self.

If you have an inner sense that your mind is satisfied only with true ideas, you will be willing to share your ideas with others, to literally test them in the marketplace. By examining and re-examining our ideas in this way, not merely intellectually but with our whole being, we will gradually understand what certainty is and why we can have inner peace only to the degree that our ideas have been developed to the state of adequacy, to the point of truth and certainty.

Chapter 23: **The Attitude of Studentship**

Many people use the word GROWTH in a very unconscious and confused way. They have a vague feeling about the word. But feelings are only the beginning of the possibilities of growth. They must be developed into clear ideas. Otherwise, they are merely associated with imaginations.

One of the first requirements for self-growth is an attitude of studentship. Do you have a desire to grow? Very good. Do you discover that your desire does not lead to results? Very frustrating. What may be missing is the attitude of studentship. You may assume that you are already quite developed inwardly.

This is a totally inadequate assumption and makes any real growth impossible because it is an erroneous ego attitude. If you begin to think of yourself consciously as a student, then the growth direction can open up for you. The ego is a cover-up for our inferiority. As a result of it, we either believe that we have arrived at a high state of development or go into the polarity of thinking we are absolutely no good.

The studentship attitude is beyond these polarities (superiority or inferiority). Studentship exists when our intelligence is active rather than when our memory dominates. The open mind thinks "I am where I am. I strongly desire to improve." It has a sense of itself and of its state and begins to think actively in specific terms about improving its understanding and its knowledge. Studentship can arise only from a sense of 'I' consciousness.

When we do not have some sense of self-consciousness, then we must compare ourselves with others, either favorably or unfavorably. But our actual state has nothing to do with anyone else's state. The ego state exists when we are not in touch with ourselves intuitively. Therefore, we must compare ourselves with others. When we have the courage to live from the inner voices of our own authority, we can become students and make real progress. Then we experience a real joyfulness and a growing sense of self-fulfillment.

Chapter 24: The Cosmic Ethics of Certainty

Recently I spoke about the difficulty one of our students has in believing that certainty is attainable. This evening we finally clarified his problem. Ralph has been motivated almost all of his life by the need for approval from other people.

If others approved of him, he could then approve of himself. Instead of using his mind for his own self-enjoyment and studying its operation and how to improve it, he used his mind merely as an instrument to earn the much-longed-for affirmation from his parents, teachers, friends and colleagues. Once he gained the approval he desired, he would then lose interest in the project he had been working on.

This motivation enabled him to use only a small part of his mind. He never probed deeply enough into anything to come to certainty about it, and therefore he never intuited that anyone could attain certainty about any idea.

Certainty is attainable only if the exercise of the mind in any study or research is motivated by the right attitude and derives from the right motivation the desire to understand something for the joy of understanding, not in order to be superior to others or to gain their approval.

48

There is a cosmic ethics inherent in the very nature of man. This is not an ethics dreamed up by human beings; it is derived from cosmic laws that are expressed in human nature. The need to attain certainty is inherent in the human mind. But as we don't know how to attain it directly, we settle for the symbol of it: if others approve of us we must be all right. But this does not satisfy our essential need any more than a picture of a meal can satisfy a hungry man.

Certainty is that state of mind arrived at when one has applied one's mind objectively to any study or problem until the mind is satisfied that it truly understands. The certainty when experienced is that statement of the mind that it indeed understands and that doubt is no longer resident. This is the true authority that fulfills one completely: the authority from within one's intelligence.

Chapter 25: The Good Is the Enemy of the Better

There is a saying that the good is the enemy of the better. If you are interested in growth, you had better become familiar with the meaning of this saying.

There is a tendency in human nature to go after self-affirmation in the easiest manner possible. We accept challenge only in areas which are not too difficult, and so we may improve in certain aspects of our character while remaining weak and becoming weaker in other areas. The man with a sore leg favors the good leg. The person who is successful in business may spend almost all of his life in this realm. The individual with a talent in music, art, etc., tends to concentrate on the aspect of his or her own talented nature.

Observe this tendency in yourself. Due to buffers, you may find it very difficult to acknowledge your weak areas. Deep down within you is a sense of your weaknesses, but you have carefully hidden them from yourself. This is how the conatus, the self-preservative force in us, acts to save us from pain.

In a real work group, the other students challenge us in our weak areas. That is why growth is only possible in such a group. By ourselves we are too shielded from our inadequacies. If you have a real desire to grow, these challenges will arouse a deep struggle in you, for the old forces do not want to surrender to the awakening desire to grow.

This is your moment of truth. Will you turn again to what you previously felt gave you satisfaction and buffer out the challenge to seek something better? Or is there enough strength in your desire to grow for you to hold onto the search for a more total development?

If you hold onto the present good and turn away from the better, the good will in time become good for nothing. The decision you make now, about seeking the better and going beyond the present good, will determine the life you will have next year and the year after. The choice is yours.

Chapter 26: **The Inner Delight in Solving Problems**

The mind has many levels, ranging from very superficial to very deep. When our mind operates at a superficial level, the quality of our life is superficial; we live mainly from our senses and instincts. Our contact with others is also very superficial, and we are guided almost entirely by our emotions.

We are insensitive to the deeper hunger of our being and are inwardly unfulfilled. We buffer our feelings of not being internally fulfilled. We fill our time with superficial activities, and we see life in terms of symbols and symptoms.

Our desires are symbols of what we need inwardly, and we deal with the symptoms of our problems. Our minds are flabby because they are not exercised. Our motivation is to avoid pain, and our pleasures are merely offsets to our pain.

To gain truer fulfillment, we must exercise our intelligence (our mind). The disappointments, the problems, and challenges in life are the exercise equipment that offer us the opportunity to deepen our thinking.

The nature of problems and challenges we struggle with will determine the quality of our growth. Dealing with physical problems such as a flat tire, being late to work, etc., provides useful exercise. But problems within ourselves and with others (our thinking, our emotions, our values, our motives) are more difficult problems and compel us to open up deeper aspects of our minds. Both levels of problems are necessary for full development of our mind requirements.

Our motives in dealing with our problems, challenges, and disappointments are most important. Are we pain-motivated? If so, do we consider our problems solved when pain stops? Are we pleasure-motivated? Then we may be interested merely in offsetting our pain with pleasure, or living only from senses and instincts.

But if we are joy-motivated, desiring to find deeper and deeper fulfillment, we approach our problems with intensity, creativity and zeal. There is an inner delight in working on, delving into, and solving problems, and we understand that the real solution of problems is not in external results but in the clarification of our thinking.

Chapter 27: The Miracle of Sharing Our Ideas

According to Gurdjieff, the highest state of human development is objective consciousness. If you have attained this level of clarity in any area, your ideas will be crystal clear because you have studied them through to the point of certainty. When you have attained certainty, you can share your ideas freely and with sureness. You can hear contrary ideas and not be upset.

You enjoy sharing your ideas and enjoy hearing the response of others to them. And if others have different ideas, you can study their ideas objectively. You can see what may be valid in their thinking and, as a result, enlarge your own ideas. Or if the other individual is confused you can see where the confusion is and help the other.

An idea which is truly objective can be shared, and sharing is different from merely bringing your ideas out to others with no interest in their thoughts. If you can't share your ideas, if you must be secretive about them, or if you insist that others accept your ideas without questioning them, then your thinking lacks certainty. There are elements of doubt, confusion and uncertainty.

The tendency to be secretive, to do things without being interested in hearing what others have to say, leads to isolation. Isolated thinking is rooted in fear ... fear that our uncertainty may be exposed and we may have to face it.

Then the law of inertia operates. There is a great resistance to overcoming the inertia of the mind which is not trained to seek self-improvement. Isolation leads to stagnation. And stagnation leads to the death of our intelligence. Without an active intelligence, we become no more than passive machines, only capable of bodily movement.

When we force ourselves to share our thoughts to experience thinking together, and to break through the wall of fear which produces isolation, we go through strong pains; but these are growing pains. In time, these pains come to an end and are replaced by an active joy within ourselves. Then we discover the miracles that the friendship of active minds produces, and we realize that growth that is really significant is only possible when we learn the miracles of thinking together.

Chapter 28: **The True Test of Growth**

One of the most disconcerting aspects of the growth path is our inability to know whether we are growing or going backwards. Only an individual with a great deal of experience and understanding of the forces in human nature can evaluate what is going on in himself or in others.

An individual can go through a period of depression or of seeming resistance to growth. He may have a desire to be isolated, may go through unexpected outbursts of anger, and believe that he is becoming inwardly weaker. But actually the individual has become strong enough to break through buffered areas and is touching previous-ly-hidden confusions. The seeming resistance to growth may be merely a resistance to think dog-matically or to go along with external authority.

The depression may arise because old standards are disappearing and new ones have not yet been established. The isolation may indicate a need to have mores since of self. The depression may arise because old standards are disappearing and new ones have not yet been established. The isolation may indicate a need to have more sense of self.

And the anger outburst may be a release of anger that one has been afraid to express because it would produce a bad image. When I assure individuals that they are going through a growth process, they are usually shocked.

But often individuals believe they are growing, whereas all that is occurring is a relief of pain. Many individuals associate this stage of pain relief as growth and delude themselves by believing they are growing. Sometimes the work tools are used merely to satisfy some ego desire.

This is why the test of growth is determined by the work teacher or by more advanced students. For it takes a number of years of active studentship before an individual can be certain that he is growing rather than fooling himself.

Chapter 29: **To Live from Within**

Either we live by the authority that arises from our deeper intelligence, from within ourselves, or else we are dominated by external authorities, whatever they may be. The practice of 'I' consciousness strengthens our sense of our self and brings us more in touch with the voice of our real intelligence. The intelligence that understands what is truly in harmony with our being. To be guided by our true inner authority is to be free.

Dr. Frederick Kettner has stated in verse:
"Live from within,
"From without dwell never.
"Thus shall thou conquer the world forever."

To live from within is to play the game of the spirit. If not, we are in the ego game. In the ego game we are either inferior or superior, either looking down on people or looking up to them. In the ego game we are always listening to voices outside ourselves. In this game there is no real initiative, no spontaneity, no real joy.

In this game there is no real communication with anyone, or real caring for ourselves. Adequate self-caring is possible only when we are guided by the authority of our inner intelligence. When our inner authority guides us, we are neither dependent nor depended on, but are capable of true mutuality. Then we know what mutual thinking is. Growth is possible only when we follow the intuition of our deeper intelligence.

The intuition that speaks from our depth enables us to see things essentially. In this state of freedom we are neither isolated nor identified with anyone. We are then whole individuals, conscious of ourselves, with true self-respect and in 'I' consciousness. We relate to others with respect for their being and are conscious of them. Then we understand how essential it is for our growth to have interactive experiences with other individuals who are also guided by their inner intelligence.

Chapter 30: **Tools for Self-Preservation**

If you are working within yourself to discriminate between your memory patterns and your intelligence, you will see that these memory patterns are not you but merely tools that you have used in order to preserve yourself. Some of these memory tools are good. For example, you remember how to speak, walk, drive a car, and so on. These are simple tools that are clear and functional. But the problems of how to relate to ourselves, relate to others, and find a meaningful direction in life requires much more advanced knowledge.

We are not capable of dealing with life's problems clearly and adequately from memory. Your memory patterns are tools, but your intelligence is you. When our intelligence senses some problem, it has made the first step toward solving it. At this point the tendency is for the memory patterns to rush in with solutions.

With simpler problems this may be sufficient, but with more involved problems our memory tools are quite inadequate. Therefore, we must discipline ourselves to stay in our intelligence while working on the problem instead of rushing back into our memory banks.

The intelligence is creative, spontaneous, in the now, totally positive, unconcerned about our image, and deeply concerned with our real being. However, it has been inactive all of our lives. At first we find it very difficult to differentiate between memory and intelligence, and between intelligence and our everyday intellect.

One of the main disciplines in activating our intelligence is seeing things in terms of their smallest units of thought. You will be shocked in working with this discipline of specifics to observe how your thoughts are a blend of fragmentary ideas rather than simple and specific ideas. A simple idea is always clear. Blended ideas are always confused.

Chapter 31: **Training Your Mind with Simple Projects**

Do you have a tendency to start something and not follow through? Do you have a variety of projects that fall into this category and remain "unfinished projects" started yesterday, several days ago, a few weeks ago, or several years' past – projects still waiting to be concluded? This means that there is a requirement in your being to discipline your mind to bring projects to completion. The undisciplined mind is a weak and untrained mind.

Take some simple project that you have neglected. Perhaps you have a button missing on a shirt or jacket. You don't have a suitable button, and you have felt it was too much trouble to think about how to replace it. The importance in working on this problem is to train and exercise you mind. The external solution is secondary.

The important factor is the opportunity to train your mind to think. When you think with your muscles, you put in practically no mind effort. You try this and try that and often give up. But if you study the problem in your mind, it becomes a wonderful and joyful experience, for you enjoy the activity of your mind.

Be aware of your mind process. Study the possibilities. Should you go to a store that sells buttons and try to duplicate the missing button? Should you remove a button from an inconspicuous location on the garment and use that as a replacement? If you can't find a matching replacement, should you replace all the buttons? Your motive in working on this project is to develop and exercise your mind for your own sake rather than to replace the button out of image.

If you work on several projects in this way during the next few weeks, you will find your mind trained to a higher level and you will have automatically set a higher standard for yourself. One result will be that you will have more self-respect and more self-confidence.

Chapter 32: **Transforming Ambitions into Inner Aspirations**

If you desire to achieve real growth, you must be a strongly-motivated individual. Otherwise you will not have the incentive and staying power to continue on the growth path in the face of confusions, inertias, dependencies, fantasies, false ideas and other deeply-rooted obstacles. This motivation, when adequate, will express itself in the form of strong aspirations for a higher level of consciousness and of being.

If you do have the necessary energy, you must direct it toward the attainment of mental and emotional maturity, that is, toward self-reliance. If not, the energy will be directed toward outward ambitions – the desire to be liked and approved of by others, to be superior to others, to attain fame and to have power over others. The deeper the essence potential in the individual the more distressed he will be if his strong energies are turned outward.

I am thinking now of someone who has a high essence potential but has concentrated on external achievements. The more business success he attained, the more frustrated he became inwardly because his real being was not nourished. And yet he resisted going beyond the childish need to prove his superiority over others. Finally his health broke down. From the existential point of view this health decay would seem tragic, but on the grow path there are no tragedies, only opportunities. His degenerating health had a wonderful effect, for he heeded this signal from his deeper being that his energies were being wrongly utilized.

If there is in you an alive essence and if you are driven by the need for external achievements and neglect your inner character, you will find your successes hollow indeed. You will have to go through a great struggle to transform your ambitions into inner aspirations. But as you develop your spiritual nature you will come to a state of fulfillment which can never be equaled by any kind of external success.

Chapter 33: **Reality Overcomes Our Dreams**

The buffering mechanism in our mind plays many tricks on our thinking in order to spare us pain. However, at the same time it inhibits our growth.

One of the illusions that this mechanism produces in us is that spiritual growth is attained by just flowing to our essential being. Spinoza and other true spiritual teachers emphasize the great effort that is required for inner work.

Some individuals with intuitive sensitivity have heard this stated time and again in our group meetings. Yet their buffering mechanism does not allow them to hear that great discipline, great overcoming, and great self-transformation are necessary for growth.

They live with vague and dreamy feelings, and may turn to drug experiences. They never face the real problems that produce growth ... problems such as superiority, ego-hidden fears, competition, and comparison. They are incapable of having solid and meaningful relationships with others based on reality and the study of real problems.

The result is that they burrow deeper and deeper into their imaginative world of mystical fantasy. They seek contact only with other individuals who also share their fantasy and who will not challenge their spiritual imaginations. The only growth they experience is growth in illusions.

That is why only active participation in a group of reality-oriented individuals can guarantee that we shall not remain lost in our private dream world. Both the materialist and the mystic are bogged down in isolation, unable to have contact with others in the common denominator of reality.

Chapter 34: **The Pendulum Principle**

Our emotions originate from our patterns of thinking. Most of our emotions operate on the pendulum principle. The opposite ends of the pendulum range are the polarities. One of the important polarity pairs is self-indulgence and dogma.

If your childhood was spent in a home environment in which dogma prevailed, you will tend to follow that dogmatic pattern. But if something in you is repelled by that atmosphere, you will switch to the opposite polarity, which is self-indulgence. Therefore, you will tend to give in to every whim and every passing desire.

If your home environment has been one of self-indulgence, you will either duplicate that pattern or gravitate to the polarity of dogma, which is rigidity. Polarities are rooted in negative psychology. They arise as reactions to existent patterns of thinking which we sense are inadequate.

A woman in our group, who had a strong tendency toward dogmatic thinking, was raised in a home which had very little discipline. Her mother was highly self-indulgent and the home atmosphere lacked intelligent discipline. In this woman's desire to have some sense of order, she developed a set of dogmatic beliefs. When I asked whether her grandmother was dogmatic, she acknowledged that she was very much so. Perhaps her great-grandmother was self-indulgent and poorly organized. And so the pendulum tends to swing within an individual and from generation to generation in a family.

When we live under the guidance of our intelligence, we are neither self-indulgent nor rigid. There is an intelligent order in our minds which harmonizes with the order of reality in life. There is a joy, a feeling of adequacy, a sense of peace and of fulfillment. We are guided in life, not by a host of patterns which have infiltrated our memory from external influences, but by the activity of our intelligence. When we live more and more by the guidance of our innate intelligence, we live beyond the mechanical existence of memory machines.

Chapter 35: **The Homing Instinct**

To paraphrase a common saying: "Be it ever so horrible, there is no place like home." In most people there is a tendency to return to their original patterns of behavior. Let us call it "the homing instinct." There is very likely some basic pattern in your psychological make-up to which you tend to return.

The tendency to complain is a very common pattern of this kind. I shall give you an example of a woman we will call Barbara. This past summer Barbara obtained a teaching assignment in a suburban high school. After accepting it, she began to complain about how much work was needed to prepare for her classes. Recently she complained about all the reading she was required to do in preparing for a master's degree.

Barbara frequently gets herself into situations such as these in order to have a good excuse to complain. Her homing instinct induces her to follow laudable plans so that she will not feel guilty about returning to home base ... the complaining home.

Ellen, another member, has a homing instinct which also brings her to complaining. But her complaint is that she is not fulfilled. She therefore sets some goal for herself which she claims will be highly satisfying, but she does not work at it and then complains about being unfulfilled.

Robert, also a member, spends long hours as a teacher. No one else on his teaching staff spends so many extra hours. But Robert says he would like a nine-to-five job. And yet he does not have a real desire to find such a job. He has produced this situation so that he can have something about which to complain.

In order to know yourself better, you will have to observe if there is in you some deeply-entrenched pattern to which you tend to return. Becoming aware of it, you will observe that the pattern is rooted in your memory. As you learn how to activate your intelligence through the process of real work on yourself, then and only then is it possible to free yourself from the tyranny of childhood memory patterns.

Do you have an interest in exploring other possibilities that may awaken a higher level of spiritual intelligence that awaits you? It is truly possible to achieve a new reality, a higher level of consciousness that goes beyond personality.

Chapter 36: **The Need for Direct Self-Approval**

The need for self-approval is innate in everyone's mind. The adequate attainment of self-approval gives us a sense of inner rightness, of peace, joy, fulfillment and freedom. If we do not come to adequate self-approval directly, then we are compelled to seek it indirectly from others. If we cannot get approval from others, we try to obtain it from our imagination.

The logic of indirect self-approval works in this way: "If others affirm me, like me, admire me, adore me, look up to me, are in awe by me, praise me, I must be all right." As few individuals ever come to true self-approval, there is a mad scramble by people to get approval from others. But how to gain direct self-approval? Remember that self-approval is earned.

There must be something we have developed which brings such self-approval. Self-approval does not involve comparison of ourselves with others. It is totally self-contained. It means that we approve of our inner growth, an intuitive affirmation that we are indeed on a growth path, that we have a sense of a growth direction and are following it.

One of the basic keys for growth is the discipline of discriminating between our conditioned memory and our innate intelligence. When we are memory-directed, our intelligence is excluded and direct self-affirmation is impossible.

When we begin to listen to our intelligence, which is very difficult and yet essential, then we begin to intuit with certainty that we are on the right track. Direct and adequate self-approval is possible only when we listen to the wisdom of our intelligence. The problem is to get in touch with our intelligence.

Chapter 37: **Sex in a Spiritual Relationship**

After working in great depth during the last
five years with young people who are earnestly
seeking spiritual direction for their lives, I am
impelled to comment on the subject of sex.

For twenty years, beginning in 1931, I was a
student in what I consider the most advanced
spiritual group of this century. For thirty years,
until her death, I was married to a student in this
group. A number of young couples met each
other and were married within the framework of
this group.

Sex was considered a relatively-simple
problem and was accepted with that attitude. In
the time I was involved in this group, about fifty
couples who also had met each other in the group
were married. In this twenty-year discipleship,
not one couple who remained in the group was
divorced.

They, and my wife and I, had problems as do
married people everywhere. But we accepted the
challenge of these problems as opportunities for
growth. There were always friends who cared
deeply and with whom problems could be shared
and studied until clarity was attained.

Today, young people consider themselves more sexually sophisticated than their parents. That they are more unrestrained I will grant, but I do not consider them more inwardly free. I equate freedom with understanding, not with lack of restraint.

The sex problem is extremely complex. Therefore, I study this problem with group members only when they have made definite progress in spiritual development. Adequate sex expression is possible only between two individuals who have attained within themselves a strong spiritual foundation and a developing spiritual relationship with one another.

Sex is an integral, wonderful and joyful part of the spiritual relationship and is considered a growth experience just as much as any other aspect of the relationship. But sex not rooted in and driving from this spiritual foundation proves frustrating to any really sensitive human being.

If you are truly interested in finding the truth of the "Spirit of Life Within" then join me in the quest of the most exciting adventure: the study and examination and improvement of our own fantastic nature.

Chapter 38: **The Symbology of Hidden Desires**

Many of our desires and interests are in
reality symbols of hidden desires that we are
unwilling to acknowledge. They are daytime
dreams that are studied in a branch of cosmic
ethics which I call *symbology*. In this message I
shall tell you about a member of our group who
uncovered the meaning of her symbolic interest.

Linda had been greatly interested in, in fact
fascinated by, science fiction. She was an ardent
fan of *Star Trek* and on several occasions she had
attended the *Star Trek* conventions after this TV
serial was discontinued. She read many science
fiction stories. On various occasions we studied
the possible real meanings behind her interest in
science fiction, for Linda gradually became aware
that there were indeed hidden desires behind
these interests.

Yesterday Linda made further progress in
interpreting the involved symbolism. She now
realizes that what she really desired was to come
into more direct contact with her own deeper
intelligence. In the past she intuited that such
higher intelligence was potentially available, but
she also felt hopeless about ever releasing it. And
yet there remained within her a refusal to give up

the desire, even though she believed it could never be realized. She expressed this desire in the form of daytime dreams about super-conscious inhabitants from outer space.

What enabled Linda to understand her desire? As she has grown in understanding through the work of our group, she has begun to sense that it would be possible to release her deeper intelligence through specific disciplines. With this awakening to her real possibilities, she will gradually lose interest in science fiction. For the real thing is always better than the dream about it.

Chapter 39: Women As Individuals

In 1930 I was a student in a Spinoza Group in
Chicago, which was dedicated to applying the
principles for growth outlined by Benedict
Spinoza. During the twenty years that I was
involved in this group, there were few women
who were so dependent on approval from men
that they submerged their individuality through
their dependence. Almost all of the other women,
all in their twenties, developed their individuality
in this group. In relating to the men they
eventually married, there was ever-increasing
mutual friendship.

Today, young women are supposedly more
liberated than women of previous generations.
And yet in the several years that the Spinoza-
Gurdjieff Group has existed, I have found that the
opposite is true. It is true that women do
participate much more frequently in sexual
expression before marriage, and they certainly are
involved in a wider variety of sexual expression.
But I have found that in deeper areas of their
nature they are much more dependent upon
approval from men in order to approve of
themselves.

In my student days, more young women than
men were interested in attaining spiritual

consciousness. Today I find that comparatively fewer women than men have the strength to attain spiritual development.

Again and again I have observed women with spiritual affirmations and potential unable to stay on the growth path because of their dependence on men. A basic principle of spiritual growth is that one must attain inner adequacy as an individual before being able to relate adequately to anyone else, especially someone of the opposite sex.

Many women these days have fostered a strong rebelliousness which they confuse with individuality. But on the basis of my experience, the state of our culture at present is an enormous obstacle to young women who desire to develop their innate uniqueness.

**Chapter 40: The Discipline of Positive
Psychology**

Positive psychology is the second of the three
disciplines our group members are studying and
applying in order to acquire more consciousness.
This evening several of us were studying the
pattern in one of our students who ends up in
negative psychology. I discovered part of his
confusion, which may turn out to be the main root
of his confusion, was based upon a misunder-
standing of how to solve a problem in one's
nature. He attempted to find out why he couldn't
be in positive psychology rather than how to be
positive-oriented.

But there was a subtle trick in his logic. He
was actually attempting to rationalize his
inadequacies rather than acknowledging them as
errors and putting in the effort to improve his
understanding. He was encouraged to come to a
decision to go ahead with a new attitude rather
than explain why he was confused. Intellectually
he was able to see and affirm this.

We will now see how well he can apply this
idea. If he falls back into his old pattern, he will
be reminded of the new insight. The habit of
negative psychology is one of the main
hindrances to growth. Our ego seeks to find out

how to go ahead without clarity. The ego is past-minded and close-minded. Our intelligence is open-minded, able to wonder, outgrow negative beliefs, and come to new understanding.

I must repeat again that negative psychology is rooted in fear. And yet this fear is not real. It exists only in our imagination. Therefore, to come to positive psychology, it may be necessary to have the courage to share our inner fears with other students in order to free ourselves. The sharing of our secret fears is very often the first step needed to come to positive psychology.

Chapter 41: **Beyond the Level of Life**

One of the fundamental points to understand about the work required for growth, and this Gurdjieff emphasizes, is that, it does not begin at the level of life but originates from a different level. Many individuals who believe they are interested in growth attempt to go about it as they would approach any other project, whether it is working on one's job, studying for some profession, designing a building, or composing music.

The path of spiritual growth cannot be attempted successfully in this way. The desire for true growth must originate from a source in the individual which he or she has very likely never worked with before … his or her essential nature.

Just about everything we do on the level of life deals with personality and physical survival. The level of life relates to money, power over others, and approval from others, sensory pleasures, intellectual pleasures, the inferiority-superiority complex, and the instinct for survival. All of these relate to the realm of ordinary experience.

But the work for growth relates to the level of one's inner being. It is not motivated by any other desire but the inner hunger for essential self-fulfillment. It brings no external rewards; it satisfies no instincts; it does not appease the senses.

The work for growth arises from a deeper self-awareness of the hunger to gain self-mastery and to liberate oneself from the bondage of emotions. One must be aware that there are two distinctly separate sides to man's and woman's nature: the essential and the existential. The essential represents the content of life; the existential is the framework. Therefore, if you have a genuine desire to grow, you must learn that these two aspects of your nature exist, that they are separate, and that the spiritual is the side that must be intuitively clear if you are to attain a truly fulfilled level of life, a life beyond the level of ordinary existence.

Chapter 42: Objective Self-Observation of Our Emotions

One of the basic keys to inner freedom is explained by Spinoza in this way: "When we are able to come to a clear idea of any passion – anger, fear, envy, greed, ambition, and so on – the passion ceases."

Our problem is: how can we come to a clear idea of any emotion? To accomplish this we must use a scientific approach with ourselves as the object of study.

The first step is to observe ourselves without judgment and without attempting to do anything about what we observe. This is an extremely difficult 'I' discipline because we have been programmed by imitating other people's values and by our own experiences. As a result, we exist as automatons without any real self-consciousness.

Writing what you observe is a highly successful aid in self-observation because this activates the mind. Writing is a form of communication, and communication originated in a more advanced part of the mind. As you practice self-observation (again I repeat, endeavoring to do so without judgment and without attempting to change your character), a law of the mind comes into operation. As Spinoza states: "Any confused emotion ceases to be a passion when we come to a clear and distinct ideas of it." Self-observation helps to bring us to inner freedom, which exists when our intelligence is active and adequate.

A simple example of this law is evident when you are angry. Attempt to observe yourself when anger is working in you. Turn your attention from the person or object that you believe causes your anger and focus on your state. You will find that the anger will lessen or disappear, for your intelligence is now being activated.

As you continue with the discipline of self-observation, you will find yourself gradually being released from the tyrannical hold of self-judgment and slowly you will come to clear ideas about your character.

Chapter 43: Positive Attitude-Growth in Facing Problems

We all have problems in our lives. Our attitude in facing these problems determines whether we can grow through working on them and also determines the adequacy with which we work.

A problem can be for the mind what exercise is for the body. Some people do exercises in a perfunctory manner and therefore gain nothing from performing them, because there is no enthusiasm or sense of self in their performance. A problem can also be approached routinely or even negatively, and no inner gain follows.

The first requirement for an adequate solution is that the problem be acknowledged with a positive attitude. Once our mind acknowledges that there is a problem, the problem can be faced directly. Otherwise, we look at the problem negatively, as something that must be gotten away from, buffered, avoided, and so on.

If you have a problem, whether it is external to you or within you, can you acknowledge the existence of the problem? Can you think and say, "I have this problem," or "This is a problem for me."? The problem may be complex, but your idea that you have a problem will then be simple.

Gregory Grover

If you can say, "I have a money problem" or "I have a family problem" or "I have an inferiority problem" this may be a simple idea. But if you imagine, "I have a problem about money and it will take too much effort to face it" or "I know that I have a heavy family problem and I will run away from it," you are in negative psychology. The emotions are now in control and the problem has not been brought to the level of conscious study.

The dictionary defines a problem as an unsettled matter demanding solution or decision and requiring considerable thought or skill for its proper solution or decision. Do you face your problems with negative psychology? Or do you acknowledge them directly and openly with your intelligence? If you acknowledge them with your mind, then you can begin to study them and grow through them.

Made in United States
North Haven, CT
12 September 2022

23991761R00059